"May the God of hope fill you with all joy and peace." Rom. 15:13

Blessings to you!

Martha Kalechman

Living in His Light

Experiencing the Presence of Jesus along Life's Journey

Martha Kalichman

Foreword by David C. MacDonald, D.O.

Copyright © 2014 Martha Kalichman.

All rights reserved. No part of this book may be used or reproduced by any means, graphic, electronic, or mechanical, including photocopying, recording, taping or by any information storage retrieval system without the written permission of the publisher except in the case of brief quotations embodied in critical articles and reviews.

Scripture taken from the Holy Bible, NEW INTERNATIONAL VERSION®. Copyright © 1973, 1978, 1984 by Biblica, Inc. All rights reserved worldwide. Used by permission. NEW INTERNATIONAL VERSION® and NIV® are registered trademarks of Biblica, Inc. Use of either trademark for the offering of goods or services requires the prior written consent of Biblica US, Inc.

Scripture taken from the New King James Version. Copyright © 1979, 1980, 1982 by Thomas Nelson, Inc. Used by permission. All rights reserved.

Scripture taken from The Living Bible copyright © 1971 by Tyndale House Foundation. Used by permission of Tyndale House Publishers Inc., Carol Stream, Illinois 60188. All rights reserved. The Living Bible, TLB, and the The Living Bible logo are registered trademarks of Tyndale House Publishers.

Scripture taken from the King James Version of the Bible.

WestBow Press books may be ordered through booksellers or by contacting:
WestBow Press
A Division of Thomas Nelson & Zondervan
1663 Liberty Drive
Bloomington, IN 47403
www.westbowpress.com
1 (866) 928-1240

Because of the dynamic nature of the Internet, any web addresses or links contained in this book may have changed since publication and may no longer be valid. The views expressed in this work are solely those of the author and do not necessarily reflect the views of the publisher, and the publisher hereby disclaims any responsibility for them.

Any people depicted in stock imagery provided by Thinkstock are models, and such images are being used for illustrative purposes only.
Certain stock imagery © Thinkstock.

ISBN: 978-1-4908-6118-0 (sc)
ISBN: 978-1-4908-6119-7 (e)

Library of Congress Control Number: 2014920937

Printed in the United States of America.

WestBow Press rev. date: 12/04/2014

Contents

Foreword ix
Acknowledgments xi
Walking in the Light xiii

1. On Track 1
2. Connected by a String 4
3. Waiting for God's Best 7
4. Here Comes the Son 13
5. At the Feet of Jesus 17
6. A Husband's Victory over Breast Cancer 23
7. Birthday Flowers 39
8. Getting to the Root of the Matter 42
9. Signs from the Great Matchmaker 45
10. Lifted Burdens 49
11. God Provides 53
12. Memory of Hope 56
13. What Happens When I Go Home? 60
14. The Salute 65
15. A Mother's Journey Home 68
16. The Bells Rang for Joy 90
17. Without a Doubt 92

Notes 95

To all who are seeking the One True Light

"When Jesus spoke again to the people, he said, 'I am the light of the world. Whoever follows me will never walk in darkness, but will have the light of life.'"
John 8:12 (NIV)

Foreword

Spiritual Ebenezers

Most people attribute good and bad situations in life to either luck, predestination, or "just the way it is." Without a belief in a Creator who is concerned about the affairs of humanity, there is no hope. The Christian worldview believes there is a God who has revealed His creative power and reliability through creation. In addition, Jesus became the bridge of hope between a fallen world and our Creator...and this belief in Jesus brings hope.

Prayer is the invisible language and means of communicating with God. Prayer can either be your steering wheel in life or your spare tire. I have had the privilege of walking the roads of life with Martha and her husband, Michael. I can assure you that prayer is Martha Kalichman's steering wheel.

In *Living in His Light,* Martha shares stories about God's intervention in her family and others. Her stories are not stories of avoiding tough situations but stories of God's sustaining presence *through* situations. My hope and faith in God was renewed by reading her stories.

Ebenezer is an Old Testament word for God's providence. Ebenezer is a strange word. Most people automatically think of the Christmas character, Ebenezer Scrooge, when asked what this word means. This word is found in a familiar hymn, *Come, Thou Fount of Every Blessing,* composed by the 18th century Methodist Pastor, Robert Robinson. If you are like many, you have probably sung this song for years without understanding what the word "Ebenezer" means.

The term actually comes from Old Testament Scripture. An Ebenezer is a memorial stone set up by Samuel to commemorate the divine assistance to Israel in their great battle against the Philistines, whom they totally routed (I Samuel 7:7-12). Literally speaking, an Ebenezer is a "stone of help," a reminder of God's presence. In Malachi 3:16, there is a reference to a "book of remembrance" of those who speak about God.

Martha's stories of God's providential involvement in life are *Spiritual Ebenezers* that remind us of God's providence. Her stories provide hope that there is a God who is concerned about the affairs of life. They remind us to make prayer our steering wheel in life, rather than the spare tire.

David MacDonald, D.O.
Family Physician

Acknowledgments

The Lord has led me to write this book through the support and insight of many. I am thankful for my dear husband, Michael, who lovingly and faithfully walks with me in this journey of life. My gratitude goes to those who so willingly offered advice, assistance, and encouragement—my daughter, Sarah, and friends, Liz Forman, Barbara Baranowski, June Keene, Beverly Vandevender, Kay Walsh, and Bobbie Yagel. I am thankful for those who graciously allowed me to share their stories. Most importantly, I thank the Lord for shining His light on my path, for keeping me on track, and for revealing that He is "the Light of the world" (John 8:12, NIV).

Walking in the Light

It is a new day. None of us know what experiences it may bring, but life's lessons have taught me to be on the lookout for God's presence. He reveals Himself to each of us in His own perfect ways.

As I face each day, I wonder what He will do next. Will He open my eyes to see life with a different perspective? Will He open my ears and fine tune what I hear? Will He change the rhythm of my heart, making it in tempo with His?

Sometimes He reveals His presence in subtle ways. Sometimes it's with His shining light. And as my friend Liz says, "Sometimes it's with *neon* signs." But whatever way He chooses, I know I don't want to miss it.

If we race ahead of Him on this path of life, we may overlook those signs. Distractions of the world may take us on a journey away from God, and we may miss those signs. However, if we stay in step with Him, a great adventure awaits us.

May the testimonies in this book encourage you and strengthen your faith. Whatever experiences life brings your way, may you, too, know the reality of God's loving and never-ending presence.

Martha Kalichman

Chapter 1

On Track

"Oh Jesus, you really *are* real!"

Bursting with laughter, I raced home. I yearned to open the pages of my Bible. I could hardly wait to read more about the One I had seen. Months before, He had beckoned me to walk with Him every day on the nearby railroad tracks.

At age sixteen, I found much solace after school while walking on the tracks extending past my family's old home. Many questions about life surfaced in the quiet time. What would I spend my future doing? Did I really want to pursue nursing as I had dreamed about since age seven? Whom would I marry?

As I walked on the straight and narrow path between the tracks, I poured out my heart to Jesus. I shared about the daily struggles I experienced with school, friends, and family—the typical challenges that many teenagers face. After I sent out my prayers, I turned around to walk home. During this time, I listened to the Lord's impression on my heart. I did this day after day, even when it rained or snowed.

While walking one sunny day in March, I was praying about my familiar list. Suddenly, at a short distance from me stood a man robed in white. Surprisingly, I had no fear. Instead, I became consumed with joy! A brilliant, glowing brightness shone around Him. No details of His face were revealed to me, but without a doubt, I knew it was Jesus. His visual appearance lasted for a brief time, but I was forever changed!

After I arrived home, I scurried to my room and read ten chapters in the book of Matthew. I earnestly wanted to tell somebody about my experience, but suspecting my parents would be skeptical, I didn't tell them. Having never heard of this happening to anyone before, I even hesitated to tell close friends. For months I kept it to myself— I did not want to risk the possibility of tarnishing this life-changing event with any negative comments. Eventually, I shared my story with others, realizing it might bring hope to some who were searching for the reality of Christ.

While in college, I met Michael. When we married two years later, we chose to have our August wedding on my parents' lawn, not far from the railroad tracks. Even though the sun beat down upon all who gathered to witness our wedding, a cloud moved over us during the ceremony, bringing a reprieve from the hot rays.

Years later, several verses from the book of Exodus caught my attention. "By day the Lord went ahead of them in a pillar of cloud to guide them on their way..."[1]

As Michael and I discussed that verse, I wondered, *Did the Lord send the cloud during our wedding, indicating His presence in our lives?* With my new perspective, I realized that the cloud coverage hovered over the nearby railroad tracks, too—the place where my life had been transformed and where I had first prayed for the man I would marry.

As Michael and I follow the Lord, He continues to reveal His presence to us. We now live far away from the path where the Lord called me to walk with Him each day, but the message I received years ago is forever etched in my mind: "You will seek Me and find Me when you seek me with all your heart."[2]

Chapter 2

Connected by a String

My uncle's phone call was unexpected. "My dad's old violin isn't playable right now," he said, "but I'd like to pass it down to Josh because he's the only one in the family who can play it."

I hardly knew what to say. My grandfather grew up in a poor family and had bought the violin with his own money when he was fifteen-years old. He played it during his young adulthood, but that was all I knew about that part of his past.

My grandfather died when I was a child. His death marked the beginning of conflicts between by father and his brothers. As I watched my son, Josh, grow into a talented violinist, it became my heart's desire for him to play the violin that my grandfather once played. With my uncle's phone call, the work of the Lord's almighty hand now revealed itself in my uncle's desire to give the treasured gift to my son. His willingness to give up the violin that held tangible memories of his father was a blessing.

Josh, a college student majoring in music at that time, was thrilled to learn he was to receive his great-grandfather's violin. Together we made the two-hour drive to my uncle's house. During the trip, Josh commented, "I wonder what his words 'not playable' and 'in pieces' really mean."

"Who knows, but if it only has minor problems, maybe you could play *Amazing Grace*, I said. "I know that's one of his favorite hymns."

When we arrived at my uncle's house, my aunt handed the case containing the violin to Josh. As he carefully opened it, I quickly noticed the wood wasn't broken. The bridge held one string, and a tuning peg was missing. Scratches penetrated through the thin coat of varnish, but in my eyes it had priceless beauty. Josh tightened the one string and took out the bow. He began to play a few notes and then gradually started playing *Amazing Grace*.

I tried to hold back the tears as Josh played the favorite hymn—on one string! Just as the one string was essential for my son to play the violin, the Lord was the essential string that had mended the previously torn relationships between our families.

As I listened to the sweet sound of the violin, I recalled the words of the hymn: "Amazing grace, how sweet the sound." By God's grace the ability to play the sweet sound that had flowed through my grandfather's fingers now streamed through the fingers of his great-grandson. Even though Josh never knew his great-grandfather, the Lord

Living in His Light

had provided a precious bond. I realized the violin was only a symbol of the magnitude of God's blessing. The talent He had given to both my grandfather and my son was the true gift.

Chapter 3

Waiting for God's Best

"Oh, Lord, if you want us to move, why is it taking so long to sell our house?" My husband and I were excited about his opportunity for a job transfer to Richmond, Virginia. The timing was perfect in many ways. The main one being that our son had just graduated from high school. In several months he would be moving anyway to a new college environment. We knew our thirteen-year-old daughter would face disappointment when leaving her friends, but we perceived the Lord had a purpose for her with this move as well. Although we had enjoyed living in Chesapeake, Virginia, we now welcomed the chance to return to Richmond where we lived years before.

While preparing our home to go on the market, I packed away knickknacks and removed most of the pictures and magnets covering our refrigerator but left one—the magnet from the *Mom's in Touch International* prayer organization.

Living in His Light

The housing market was booming that year. We were thrilled that the season for selling a house was at its prime. Typically, in our neighborhood during that time, houses were sold within two weeks.

Many doors had opened for this move, so I felt confused when family after family traipsed through our home, but made no offers. Remarks from their realtors were positive, but "it wasn't exactly what they were looking for."

After a month we re-evaluated our situation and lowered the price. But week after week, although many people continued to look at the house, no contracts came.

Weariness and discouragement remained ever present in my mind as the frequent barrage of potential buyers looked and left our house. The constant pressure of keeping the house clean and maintaining the yard added to the stress. Knowing that my husband would soon have to report to his new job in Richmond caused further frustration.

I had prayed and prayed for the right buyer to come. And then one Saturday morning, I began praying with a different perspective. "If you want us to move, Lord, then surely you must have a plan for selling our house." Suddenly, it no longer mattered to me when we sold it. I simply surrendered the whole situation to Him, knowing that in His perfect time, He would bring a buyer. Great peace accompanied that relinquishment.

Later that morning our realtor called. "I have a client who wants to see your house this afternoon."

"That'll be fine," I said with renewed hope.

Waiting for God's Best

After lunch our family left the premises as we frequently did when someone came to see our home. An hour later we returned to discover the couple still inspecting our house and seriously considering buying it! We soon learned they had recently traveled back to the United States from Japan where the husband worked for the Navy. While living in Japan his wife had regularly attended a *Mom's in Touch International* prayer group. When they saw the magnet on our refrigerator, they perceived it as a confirmation that our home was to be their new home.

I suddenly realized that only a few hours before, I had totally relinquished our house to the Lord. I was in awe that on that same day, He brought the perfect buyers to our house! While He prepared the timing of their arrival, He had prepared me to totally trust Him.

All went well with our move to Richmond. We had hoped to purchase a house that we could move into directly. However, finding one with the right price and location became challenging, so we opted to rent an apartment for several months.

Each time we looked at a house that seemed suitable, conflicts arose—either someone offered more than we did, or hidden problems with the house surfaced, which home inspections later revealed. After three times of failed contracts, my frustration escalated with this predicament. Many of our belongings were in storage, including winter clothes. We had presumed we wouldn't need them while we lived in the apartment for a brief time. But now, winter approached. Once again, I could not understand the Lord's timing.

Due to our growing impatience about the situation, we decided to re-evaluate a house we had seen previously. Through various people, this house had come to our attention repeatedly in the prior month. It needed obvious repairs that were reflected in the low price, but we wondered if the Lord had reasons for us to buy this house that we didn't understand. After a thorough tour, we signed a contract and indicated that our final decision would depend on a home inspection.

Several days later the inspector came to the house. He detected many problems that we had not—some minor, some major. We left feeling confused, questioning the Lord, "What are You guiding us to do?" We wanted to be obedient, and yet we perceived that the repairs would breed burdensome expenses.

That evening at a cookout given by the company where Michael works, we met some of his co-workers and their wives. While chatting with one couple, we mentioned that we had a contract on a house but added, "We don't have a firm peace about it yet."

The lady looked at me and asked, "Do you think that's the house the Lord wants you to have?"

"Well, it seems He has led us to it a couple of times, so maybe it is."

"But don't you think He wants to give you the best?" I pondered that question for a while. Perhaps this wasn't the house He wanted us to have—maybe not His best for us.

That night, neither Michael nor I slept well. Peace eluded us. The next day Michael called our realtor with our decision. "We want to cancel the contract due to the many problems discovered during the home inspection," he said. The realtor agreed to follow through with our request.

Relieved to be free from the contract, our peace returned. Our perspective totally changed about the urgency to find a house. We were ready to be content in our cozy apartment. It no longer mattered how long we needed to stay there.

A week later we learned of a house for sale by the owner in a neighborhood that was in a perfect location for us—close to Michael's office and our daughter's school. We called the owner and asked to schedule an appointment to see it. Since stiff competition in the housing market continued, we did not have high hopes.

When we arrived at the house the next day, the owners graciously welcomed us. Although they had received many calls after our call, they had chosen not to allow anyone else to see the house before we did. We learned they had experienced a similar situation and had difficulty finding a house when they had moved to Richmond twelve years before.

As we walked through the house, I noticed several decorations that were like ones we possessed. One of the pictures hanging on a wall was identical to one we owned. The words from Scripture on it, "Love is patient, Love is kind,"[1] revealed God's care in His direction. No repairs were necessary, and everything on our mental list of priorities was evident in this house. Even the price was the same as the selling price of the one we sold in Chesapeake. Without a doubt, we knew the Lord had led us to this home— His best for us.

We have now lived in our home through many seasons of life. The Lord has reminded us in trivial and significant experiences that He always wants what is best for His children.

Chapter 4

Here Comes the Son

"Hi, Mom. Remember when Dad wished that Michael would get a deer when they went hunting?" I asked during a phone call while on vacation with my husband.

"Oh yes, I sure do," Mom replied.

"Well, he finally got one!"

We had been traveling on the Pennsylvania Turnpike near Pittsburgh one beautiful October morning heading to Ohio to visit our son, Josh. I had finished reading a devotional by Oswald Chambers with a Scripture reference from Mark 9:2—"Jesus took...and led them up on a high mountain apart by themselves."[1]

Moments later, a large deer suddenly appeared at the top of an embankment. Traffic was busy, but no cars were nearby at the time. Trying to anticipate the deer's action, Michael stepped on the brakes. But before he could stop, the deer leapt down the hill. With a loud thud, the deer fell on the hood of our van without leaving even a scratch on the windshield! His injured body then flew off and landed two lanes over. The van's engine sputtered, causing Michael to pull onto the shoulder.

Within minutes, a man driving a pick-up truck pulled over. After he asked if we were okay, he inquired, "Do you want the deer?"

In unison Michael and I answered, "No!"

During a break in the flow of the traffic, the man ran across the highway to the deer. Grasping its antlers, he dragged it to the shoulder of the road and waited with us for the policeman to arrive.

Several hours later after a tow-truck excursion followed by a taxi ride, Michael and I reached the local airport, the closest place to rent a car. For the rest of our trip, our eyes scanned the road for deer trying to escape the hunters on that first day of hunting season.

During the following week, we enjoyed being a part of our son's world, meeting his friends and his church family. Several of his friends shared their deer stories, and I began to see our accident and being free of injury with new eyes.

By midweek, we learned that the replacement parts for our van had not arrived as scheduled. If the repair work could not be finished by the end of the week, an additional trip would be necessary at a different time. Michael and I became annoyed by the inconvenience and expense this situation caused.

Early the next morning, I awoke with a startling thought. *How could I complain about a return trip when God had spared us from any injury in the accident? We should rejoice in being alive!* Clearly, along with the repair of the van, God had repaired my attitude. Instantly, I felt overjoyed that Michael and I were healthy and capable of traveling back.

Two weeks later when we left for the six-hour trip to Pennsylvania, clouds filled the sky. Pouring rain soon followed and accompanied us for the entire trip. I remembered the milepost of the deer encounter and pulled out my camera while we drove closer to the site. But the rain and the moving windshield wipers distorted the view.

When we reached three miles from the area, the rain suddenly stopped. I looked through the camera lens as we approached the location of the accident. To our astonishment, the sun burst through the clouds over the mountains! Speechless, Michael and I looked at each other. Tears welled up in our eyes. In that moment, the brilliant sunlight reminded us of the protection the Son had shone over Michael and me two weeks before.

After we rode past the site, the sun immediately vanished behind the clouds. We recalled the devotional I had read the morning of the accident. Oswald Chambers had concluded his writing for that day with "The moments on the mountaintop are rare moments, and they are meant for something in God's purpose."[2] The Lord had truly taken us to a high mountain to reveal His presence.

When we arrived at the car shop, the mechanic informed us of the repairs done. "The air conditioner and all of the hoses with it needed to be replaced," he said. Michael and I laughed. During the previous summer, minor problems with the air conditioner had occurred, but we postponed the repair due to the expense of the job. Not only had God protected us, but He also had taken care of every detail, even blessing us with a new air conditioner that the insurance company covered.

"Here's your key—have safe travels home," the mechanic said.

Hand in hand, Michael and I walked to the van. I noticed the license plate letters—"JCV...remember, Michael, what that meant to us when we bought the van years ago?"

"Jesus Christ's Victory," we said together.

We climbed into the van. Once again, those letters reminded us of the One who truly holds the key for providing victories in life. And if needed, He repairs misaligned attitudes, enabling us to receive His blessings.

Chapter 5

At the Feet of Jesus

My husband and I are blessed with two children who are now adults. Having never had any problems with pregnancies and delivery of healthy babies, I haven't grasped the level of pain that many women endure with a miscarriage or loss of a baby at birth. However, through the story of my friend Liz, the Lord has given me a glimpse of that painful season of life that many encounter. Even in the darkness of my friend's loss, the Lord revealed signs of His compassion and sovereignty, bringing her much comfort.

It was the summer of 1994. Liz and her husband, Greg, were expecting their long-hoped-for, second child. Along with that excitement came the opportunity for them to move from Charlotte, North Carolina, to Richmond, Virginia, where Greg had accepted a new job.

During Liz's third trimester, she, Greg, and their three-year-old daughter, Elizabeth, packed their belongings and headed to Richmond. Liz had found an obstetrician

Living in His Light

through the Yellow Pages, trusting the Lord would help her pick the doctor He wanted her to see. She soon realized He had guided her to the right one when the doctor ordered an ultrasound.

"Would you like to know if the baby is a boy or girl?" her doctor asked.

Having already had this test done before in Charlotte, Liz informed him that the insurance company would not pay for an additional one.

"Don't worry, it's on me," he said. His kindness exceeded that of any doctor she had ever known.

After having another ultrasound, the technician led her back to the doctor's office, encouraging her to have a seat next to his desk. When the doctor entered the room, his words startled Liz. "We have some problems here, Liz. Where is your husband?" She gave him the phone number but wanted the doctor to begin telling her the results. While they waited for her husband's arrival, she and the doctor viewed the ultrasound. He gently described her baby's suffering—skull and brain problems, spina bifida, clubbed feet, and heart problems. The list went on and on, tearing apart the hopes and dreams she and her husband once had for this child. In those moments Liz felt her world shatter.

"I think your baby is suffering from a genetic condition called *Edwards Syndrome (Trisomy 18),*" her doctor said. "I know a specialist I'd like you to see."

During the months between August and November, Liz sensed the Lord holding her hand as she faced each

At the Feet of Jesus

new day. She prayed for a miracle as she felt the presence of new life within her. She continued to have a growing bond with the daughter she carried. Yet, in the midst of the heartbreak, the Lord enabled Liz to relinquish her baby to Him. He poured His peace over her.

Liz's young daughter, Elizabeth, was aware that her mother was going to have a baby, and Liz wondered how to explain about her baby sister's problems. One evening during their bedtime ritual of reading stories and saying prayers, she thought of an explanation. "Elizabeth, sometimes when babies are born, they go straight to live with Jesus. And sometimes we know if that's going to happen, and sometimes we don't." Her daughter listened while Liz continued. "We happen to know that baby Frances is going to live with Jesus. It's a perfect place to live, and one day when we go to heaven, we'll see her again." Elizabeth readily accepted this news—clearly showing childlike faith that Jesus wants us all to have.

Three days after her due date, baby Frances was born into the heavenly realms. She went directly from the warmth and love of her mother to the warmth and love of her heavenly Father. Although this was not the miracle that Liz had hoped for, she soon realized that through the Lord's sovereignty He had delivered baby Frances from misery. He had spared Liz and Greg from emotional despair of watching their child suffer.

Liz and Greg had the opportunity to hold their dear baby and baptize her. Liz nestled Frances, bundled in her baby blanket. When the time came to let go, she felt the Lord's peace and sensed He was already holding Frances.

When Liz was taken to her room, surprisingly, she began to perceive that Frances was still with her—words strongly came to her mind. "Look for me, Mama. You'll see me in the gray ballerina on the left." Liz didn't know what that meant, but she knew she had heard a compelling voice within her mind. Wanting to keep the memory alive, she wrote the words in her diary.

How strange it seemed to Liz to be shopping for burial clothes for her newborn baby. Before the funeral Liz and Greg had a chance to see Frances dressed in a dainty white gown and booties. A pretty bonnet laced her sweet face. In Frances's tiny hands, she held a small piece of her big sister's blanket.

Three days later Liz and Greg traveled to South Carolina for the burial of their daughter. On the morning of the funeral when they approached the cemetery, the sight of the little white coffin brought heartbreak and many tears. The rays from the bright sun streamed down on the yellow roses that stretched across the top of the casket.

After the preacher's message, Liz read Psalm 121 from the little pink Bible she had bought for Frances. She held onto the promise of the words—"I lift up my eyes to the hills, where does my help come from? My help comes from the Lord, the maker of heaven and earth."[1]

As Liz and Greg knelt by the casket, they said the Lord's Prayer. The simple service brought them much

At the Feet of Jesus

comfort, and yet saying "good-bye" and leaving the cemetery deeply pulled at their hearts.

In the days ahead, life moved on for their family. The Lord continued to bless them with His strength and presence. Two years later, He blessed them with the birth of a healthy baby girl, Anne. And then in the following year, the Lord blessed Liz with an experience that would transform her faith by leaps and bounds.

It was during the Christmas season when Elizabeth was six-years-old. With excitement, she and her mother prepared for the annual Christmas pageant at their church. This year it was even more spectacular since Elizabeth was playing the part of one of the two cherubs who knelt at Mary's feet.

While Liz helped her daughter get ready before the performance, a typical mother-versus-daughter argument occurred regarding what Elizabeth should wear with her cherub costume. She could choose to wear either white socks or ballet slippers. Since she possessed the latter, she had made up her mind. The other cherub wore white socks. Liz was determined the girls should match, but her daughter was equally determined to wear her slippers.

As the procession of the pageant began, Liz felt her emotions stirring. Struggling to keep her composure, she strived to hold the video camera steady. But inside she was sobbing while she watched Elizabeth kneel at Mary's feet. Liz felt puzzled by her heightened emotions. *What's different this time?* she wondered. *Perhaps I'm just being a proud mother.*

Later that day while Liz and Elizabeth viewed the video of the pageant, a bright, blinding flash of light appeared before Liz, causing her to sit straight up on the sofa. Feeling unsteady on her feet, she crawled to the television, tears pouring down her face. Not wanting to alarm Elizabeth, she tried to explain to her that she was okay.

A distinctly clear voice in Liz's mind echoed the same words she had heard after baby Frances was born. "Look for me, Mama. You'll see me in the gray ballerina on the left."

Liz rewound the video to view the scene over and over. Fixing her eyes on her daughter, she watched this little cherub kneeling with her hands folded in prayer. Stunned, she continued to stare at Elizabeth. Her daughter, with her ballet slippers on, knelt at the left side facing Mary who was holding Baby Jesus. Gazing at her costume, Liz realized afresh that it was the most beautiful shade of silvery gray.

Through God's awesome and mysterious ways, He shed His light and peace over Liz. He gave her assurance of His reality and an affirmation that baby Frances was truly healed. Without a doubt, Liz knew that her precious baby was sitting at the feet of Jesus in heaven.

Chapter 6

A Husband's Victory over Breast Cancer

"What do you think about this knot?" my husband Michael asked me. As he directed my hand to the small lump on his chest, we both pushed and tried to move it.

"Does it hurt?" I asked.

"Well, it didn't until we started pushing on it," he replied with a rueful smile. As registered nurses, we both agreed it probably wasn't anything significant but decided he should get it checked. Thus, Michael made an appointment to see the family doctor. Because the lump was firm, the doctor advised him to have a mammogram.

"This is for you," Michael said, smiling as he handed me a fresh cut carnation when he arrived home from the mammogram. "On my way out of the office the receptionist asked if I would like to pick out a flower, so I picked this one for you."

"Thank you," I said with mixed emotions. I remembered this kind gesture of the office staff from my previous visits. A container filled with carnations was located near the door for the patient to take one when leaving the office.

"So, how did the appointment go?" I asked.

"It was okay," he said. "When I waited in the x-ray room after I removed my shirt, the nurse told me, 'We have gowns if you get cold, but this is all we have.' Then, she held up a pink flowered gown! I told her I was fine—I didn't need one."

As Michael described this scene, I felt resentful that he had to endure the awkwardness of this ordeal. We compared notes of the mammogram experience—something I never would have imagined discussing with my husband. I had wondered if the x-ray could be done on a slim man such as Michael, but I learned that yes, the x-ray is indeed done the same way for men as it is for women.

Since the normal procedure during this office visit included viewing the mammogram films immediately with the radiologist, Michael had the opportunity to see the small knot. The doctor informed him that it looked suspicious and recommended that Michael make an appointment with a surgeon. Two days later he met with one.

"That lump needs to come out," the surgeon told us as Michael and I sat in his office. He explained that there is a condition in some men called *gynecomastia,* which is a benign growth, but since this knot was firm, the doctor was concerned and advised scheduling a biopsy.

The sun was rising early in the morning when Michael and I rode to the hospital for the breast biopsy. We both felt peace about the day ahead. After Michael was taken back to the operating room, I found a comfortable chair in the waiting area. But the constant distraction of the TV prompted me to look for a different area to sit. I noticed the chapel nearby, a perfect place to have some quiet time. No one else was there, yet the silence along with the sun peering through the stained-glass windows filled the chapel. I opened the large Bible that lay on the podium and turned to Psalm 34. When I read verse 10 "...but those who seek the Lord lack no good thing," my thoughts drifted to the time when Michael began seeking answers about God.

He was raised in a Jewish family, and I in a Christian home. During my teenage years, I couldn't imagine marrying someone of another faith. However, when I went to college, I met Michael. Our friendship grew, although we struggled with one major conflict—religion. When he first went to college, he had left most of the Jewish traditions behind but continued to have a strong belief in God.

As our relationship matured, Michael and I rationalized that we could love each other in spite of our different views and entered marriage with a commitment to make it work. Five years later, we were blessed with our son, Josh. While I watched him grow, I yearned to return to church and take him with me. Michael approved of my desire, and to my surprise, on the Sunday I planned to visit a nearby church with Josh, Michael decided to go, too.

On our way to the church, we passed a double-wide green trailer where a new congregation was temporarily meeting. I felt a strong nudge to go there, although I really didn't want to. I wanted to go to a church that was already organized and not going through growing pains. However, the feeling persisted as we continued down the road until I found myself convincing Michael to turn around and go to the green trailer. I hoped we weren't making a mistake, but I wondered, *Would the service be normal? Would the people be pushy in an attempt to get new members?* I earnestly wanted Michael to have a positive impression.

As we drove into the gravel parking lot, cars filled the spaces quickly. Friendly greeters welcomed us when we stepped through the front doors. We sang familiar hymns, reminding me of my childhood church where my mother had played the organ. I felt right at home. Since there were many visitors, fitting in was easy.

The minister's dynamic sermon kept Michael's attention, as well as mine. At the end of the service, I knew I wanted to become part of this church. After we attended several Sunday services, the minister came to visit us. When he discovered Michael was Jewish, he asked about his background. Then, I heard surprising words from the preacher, "Maybe you should read a book in the New Testament—the book of Mark," and then he added, "I would be very interested in knowing what you think of it." I had never considered asking Michael to read the New Testament. I had always wanted him to become a Christian, but I did not want to pressure him into that belief.

In the following days, I watched Michael spend time reading the Bible. During our conversations, he made occasional comments about the Old Testament prophecies referencing the Messiah. As he became aware of their fulfillment in the New Testament, Michael became more motivated to learn about Christ.

We continued to go to the same church in the weeks ahead. Later that year while out of town for a work-related project, Michael went for a walk one evening. On that cold, starry night God removed the darkness that had covered his eyes, and the light of Christ started to shine through. A warmth and peace that he had never experienced before consumed him.

Several weeks later during a small Sunday evening service, I watched my husband publicly profess his acceptance of Jesus as his Savior and his desire to be baptized. Although Michael and I had recited our wedding vows seven years earlier, now we were truly one with Christ. I remembered the words from Matthew 19:6 (NIV), "...what God has joined together, let man not separate." Through God's grace, He had allowed me to come back to Him with Michael by my side.

My thoughts returned to the present circumstance. With tear-filled eyes, I recalled the words we had promised on our wedding day, "To love each other in sickness and in health." Almost 30 years had passed since that time. We had faced other health problems in our family but never cancer for either of us. I reread the Scripture in Psalm 34:10 (NIV), "...but those who seek the Lord lack no good thing." Michael had sought and found Him. Surely the Lord would allow him to "lack no good thing."

After the surgeon performed the breast biopsy, he reported, "I'm almost certain the tumor is benign, but the pathology report will give us a definite answer." We thanked God, our fears disappeared, and life resumed to normal.

One in a Hundred

A few days after Michael's breast biopsy, the stress from dealing with the concerns about Michael's health had caught up with me. I yearned to feel the Lord's presence and peace; I hungered to listen to Him. While praying, I remembered a devotional Scripture I had read earlier that morning, "...let us strip off anything that slows us down or holds us back, and especially those sins that wrap themselves so tightly around our feet and trip us up; and let us run with patience the particular race that God has set before us."[1]

In the stillness of that morning I pondered that Scripture. Memories emerged of my own experiences, which were wrapped tightly around my feet slowing me down. I perceived that whenever I hold onto thoughts of bitterness and judgment towards others, I feed the wounds of resentment. As I sat quietly, I realized this sin was holding me back, preventing me from running the race the Lord has set before me.

This new comprehension of the cleansing that He requires before we can enter into prayer prepared me for the news I received minutes later when Michael called from work. "I just talked to the doctor," he said. Instantly, I sensed the seriousness in his voice. "The pathology report showed the tumor was not benign. It's cancer, Martha."

"You're kidding!" I blurted out.

"I wish I were," Michael said. "Tomorrow the doctor wants to talk with us about additional surgery."

A myriad of emotions consumed me as I tried to absorb what he was telling me. Although we were both stunned, I knew the Lord had been transforming me all morning before this alarming phone call and preparing me to pray with a pure heart.

Even though Michael and I were aware that breast cancer could occur in men, we thought it was extremely rare. However, at the appointment with the surgeon, we learned that one in every 100 cases occurs in men. As he explained the possibility of lymph node involvement, I struggled to keep my composure, wavering between fear and hope. Michael appeared calm and asked appropriate questions.

The surgeon handed us a booklet about breast cancer. While we went over the information with him, we noticed that the booklet was filled with pink pages and only referenced women. Only one percent of the cases occurs in men, but now that Michael fell into that category, the one percent personally translated into 100 percent. Since breast cancer in men typically begins with a growth in the ducts at the nipple, I realized how easily men could do self checks for this type of tumor if only they knew the need to check.

Obesity and family history are a couple of risk factors prevalently seen in men who develop breast cancer, but Michael did not fit into those categories. Before leaving the surgeon's office, Michael asked the surgeon, "Do you think there's a possibility of an error in the pathology report?"

"That's unlikely," he said. "But if you want to get a second opinion, I'll see what I can do."

Michael offered to pick up the slides at the hospital and transport them to another pathologist whom the doctor had recommended. When the surgeon made the necessary call, we all felt disappointed to learn it could take a few days before the hospital would release the slides. After the appointment, Michael and I drove to a nearby church to pray. We sat in a pew surrounded by silence in the beautiful sanctuary and recalled the Lord's reassurance several months before during a different cancer scare. We held onto the Scripture in Psalm 91:14-16 (NIV), "'Because he loves me,' says the Lord, 'I will rescue him; I will protect him, for he acknowledges My name. He will call upon Me, and I will answer him; I will be with him in trouble, I will deliver him and honor him. With long life will I satisfy him and show him my salvation.'" We carried a Bible with us into the church and decided to read from Psalm 91. After a fervent prayer time, I headed home, and Michael went back to work.

Later that day, Michael called. "You'll never believe this! The hospital called and informed me that I could pick up the biopsy slides anytime, so I'm on my way to the pathologist's office with the slides!"

When Michael returned home, he reported that the pathologist even had time to look at the slides immediately. Michael asked if he could see them, too. The pathologist agreed and kindly explained the slides while they examined them under the microscope. Although we wished the news had been different, the confirmation of an accurate biopsy report gave us peace. With Michael's own eyes, he had seen that the tumor cells were cancerous. Surgery was scheduled for the following week.

Remembering God's Promises

"If it's in the lymph nodes, it means chemotherapy." I found it hard to shake off the surgeon's words from our last appointment. Concerns that the cancer might have spread sank deeper into my thoughts. However, the next day I received an encouraging e-mail from a friend, which strongly impacted my thinking. She wrote in the last line of her note, "Let's thank God and praise Him for healing Michael and for a long cancer-free life ahead." The words *long life* struck me profoundly as I recalled the words in Psalm 91—"with *long life* will I satisfy him." The joy of the Lord instantly filled me from head to toe as I felt this was an affirmation that Michael's health would be restored.

Nevertheless, at 2 a.m. that night, I awoke with a consuming fear as I recalled what the surgeon said. Michael was sound asleep. Not wanting to waken him, I crept downstairs with an urgency to pray. Darkness engulfed me. I desperately wanted Michael to be spared of more involved treatment than the already-scheduled surgery. My heart was in turmoil, and the tears fell uncontrollably. As I cried out to the Lord with my pleas, calmness overcame me. Words began to flow nonstop through my mind.

> *Remember, remember, remember.*
> *Remember the cloud of protection I have kept*
> *over you and Michael*
> *since the day you married.*
> *Remember the distress I have protected Michael*
> *from in the past.*
> *Remember that I healed your daughter.*
> *Remember that I have protected your son.*
> *Remember that I love Michael and you and your*
> *children.*
> *Remember that Michael will live a long life.*
> *Remember My promises.*
> *Remember, remember, remember.*

Peace flooded every cell of my body. I curled up on the sofa and soon fell into a restful sleep. The next morning

I could hardly wait to share the Lord's reminders with Michael. Through the following days prior to surgery, God poured His peace over us, and our strength came from the "joy of the Lord."[2]

On the weekend before Michael's surgery, we had planned to visit friends and relatives in Virginia Beach. We looked forward to getting away for a few days. We also anticipated that our friends Marcia and George with their jovial attitudes would have a positive influence on us.

I described to Marcia that Michael's type of cancer typically begins in the breast buds near the nipple area. She looked at me and announced, "So, they're just going to 'nip it in the bud!'" We both laughed. Somehow I perceived the Lord had a sense of humor about this, too. Through Marcia's amusing words, it was another reminder that Michael would be spared of lymph node involvement—that he would be "cancer-free."

Healed by His Stripes

A sunny, August morning greeted us on the day of surgery. Michael and I spent time in prayer and then headed to the hospital holding onto the promises etched in our minds. I dropped him off at the entrance door, and Sarah and I searched for a parking space. While walking to the hospital from the parking lot, I heard, "Hey, Martha! The party's here!" To my surprise, three of my dear, prayer-warrior friends had come to sit with Sarah and me

Living in His Light

during Michael's surgery. I knew their lively personalities would help pass the time for the long day ahead.

At lunch time the "prayer warriors" accompanied Sarah and me to the cafeteria. John, another friend from church, met us there. Frequently, I glanced at my watch anticipating the arrival of 12:30—the scheduled starting time for Michael's surgery. The time slipped away, and soon I realized it was already 1:00, so we all headed to the chapel to pray. As soon as we were seated, the nurse from the operating room called me. "We're running behind schedule, but we're now ready to begin surgery," she said. Just as we were preparing to pray, my friend Rose, a nurse at the hospital, walked in the door. Once again, the Lord had His own perfect timing, making it possible for the seven of us to gather for prayer.

Later, I learned how Michael spent the time prior to surgery. A curtain hung around the brightly lit cubicle where he waited on a stretcher. He easily overheard conversations of the nurses scurrying around while they prepared patients for surgery. Until the nurses moved him to the operating room, Michael tried to tune out the voices as he recited Psalm 91 silently, bringing him much comfort.

Two hours later after the operation, I talked with the surgeon. "There was no cancer in the lymph nodes!" he announced. I was elated; Michael would be spared from chemotherapy. Sarah and I hugged each other and hurried back to the chapel to share the great news with our friends. Together, we all got on our knees, thanking the Lord for answering our prayers.

After calling our son, who lives far away, and the rest of our relatives to share the news, Sarah and I returned to the chapel to soak in the peace and joy we felt. Later during our wait while Michael was in recovery, Sarah and I browsed in the gift shop and spotted the perfect balloon. The words from Psalm 91:11—"He will command his angels concerning you to guard you in all your ways"— were written across the bottom of it.

At seven o'clock that evening, Michael was feeling well enough to go home. The nurse wheeled him to the van, and he slowly climbed in. The balloon bobbed up and down in the back of the van as a constant reminder of the Lord's promises. I inched along the highway because Michael was sensitive to the bumps in the road. The surgeon had given him prescriptions for pain medicines and for nausea, but we still needed to get them filled. I prayed all the way home he would not get sick; he never did.

I began to wonder when the pain would hit. With an incision across half of his chest, I expected impending pain, but he only felt mild soreness. After we arrived home, he sipped on ice chips and ginger ale and felt relieved that the nausea subsided. By 10:00 p.m. I was amazed when Michael said, "Before going to bed, I'd like to sing *Standing on the Promises.*" So, Michael, Sarah, and I gathered at the piano, and we all sang the favorite hymn with deep, heartfelt joy.

Along with sparing Michael of any metastases, the Lord had calmed the pain. With 34 staples lined up across his chest, amazingly, Michael only needed mild pain medication during his recovery. The pink incision looked much like a stripe, thus prompting us to recall the Scripture, "...by whose stripes ye were healed."[3]

Now seven years later, Michael's "stripe" has faded, but it will always be a reminder to us that through the Lord's suffering and sacrifice, He desires to heal us.

The Dilemma

At Michael's follow-up appointment with the surgeon, he was instructed to take a medication that blocks estrogen. This medicine works as an anticancer drug against estrogen-fed tumors, which was the case for Michael. He took the prescription from the doctor and did not question him, but we decided to pray about whether God wanted Michael to take it.

We learned that common side effects from this drug may include various cardiovascular problems. For Michael no family history of breast cancer exists, but the hereditary risk of cardiovascular disease does. Therefore, it did not seem wise for Michael to take this medication. As we prayed about this, we remembered the words in Psalm 91: "with long life will I satisfy him." But doubt tried to creep in. We wanted clear discernment that Michael was making this choice in accordance with God's plan.

A few weeks later we attended a medical healing conference at The Healing Center in Orkney Springs, Virginia. As we met and prayed with a physician, Michael briefly described his situation to him and mentioned that he had been praying about whether to take this medication. The doctor looked at Michael and said, "You're done; you don't need to take it." He then added, "You're going to live a long life." Michael and I both laughed. We had been holding onto those words through the entire ordeal, and the Lord was reminding us of them one more time—a true confirmation that Michael needed no further treatment.

Standing on the Promises

We have learned to "listen up" to the ways the Lord may choose to speak to us. Sometimes we have heard His instructions through His word. Sometimes we have heard it through silence when we open our minds to the thoughts He impresses on us. And sometimes it has been through others.

In this process of learning to be more attentive, we yearn to stand on His promises, as one of our favorite hymns profoundly reminds us.

Standing on the Promises
By Kelso Carter

Standing on the promises of Christ my King,
through eternal ages let his praises ring;
Glory in the highest, I will shout and sing,
Standing on the promises of God.

Standing on the promises that cannot fail,
When the howling storms of doubt and fear assail,
By the living word of God I shall prevail,
Standing on the promises of God.

Standing on the promises of Christ the Lord,
Bound to him eternally by love's strong cord,
Overcoming daily with the Spirit's sword,
Standing on the promises of God.

Standing on the promises I cannot fall,
Listening every moment to the Spirit's call,
Resting in my Savior as my all in all,
Standing on the promises of God.

Chorus: Standing, standing, standing on
the promises of God my Savior;
Standing, standing,
I'm standing on the promises of God.

Chapter 7

Birthday Flowers

"I finished pruning the bushes this morning," Michael announced when he came in for lunch.

"I know you're glad," I said. "Did you see all of those buds on the camellia bush?"

"Yes, but they've looked the same for months." He hesitated and then sheepishly added, "So I pruned them, too."

"You did what? This is the first year that bush has had buds!"

"Well, I figured they were never going to bloom," he said. "I didn't know they were so important to you—I'm so sorry."

I didn't want to act unappreciative of all the work he had done, but I simply could not hide my shock. I raced to inspect the bush to see if, by chance, any buds had missed the pruning shears. To my relief, I discovered three little buds hiding under some leaves. During the days ahead I continued examining the blooming progress of the precious buds. The petals were tightly bound together for weeks, and I too began to wonder if they would ever bloom.

My camellia bush brings back memories of my grandparents' small farm in southeast Virginia. I spent much time there as a child. Many afternoons after school while my mother taught piano lessons, my two brothers and I climbed into my dad's pickup truck, and he took us to visit Grandma and Granddaddy. Spending time on their farm offered a different type of education to me than the schoolbooks. Seemingly never-ending chores faced my grandparents each day.

My grandfather and I walked together in the afternoons carrying the "slop" for the pigs. They snorted and squealed, anticipating the less-than-appetizing meal. I soon learned that the pigs would contribute to many of our meals one day.

Peanut fields stretched across much of the surrounding land. Endless rows of peanut plants shared the soil with weeds that needed to be chopped. Using a hoe, I learned to release the prized plants from their entanglement.

The garden yielded many vegetables that also needed attention while they grew. However, the work was worth the efforts when the abundance of fresh produce finally reached the kitchen table.

It was fun to check on the chickens. With a basket in hand as I ran out the back door, Grandma would call to me, "When you go in the chicken yard, Martha, be sure to shut the gate behind you." Upon entering the chicken house, the clucking began with dust and feathers flying all around me. I knew if I waited while the dusty air settled, many eggs would be the reward.

Sometimes my grandmother and I would examine her camellia bush together. In blooming season, brilliant red blossoms covered it. She, like my father and grandfather also had a *green thumb*. Today, when I look at my camellia bush, it is evident I did not inherit a similar thumb, nor did my husband. But in March, the petals on one of the flowers began separating. Each day they expanded more. On March 19th, the day that would have been my dad's 83rd birthday, I was amazed to see the flower finally reach its full bloom.

For the next week, I watched another bud begin to separate. Once again, I was in awe that on March 24th, my son's birthday, the flower fully bloomed. I looked for the third bud, but it was nowhere to be found.

The blooms reminded me of God's continual care for us. He connects our family together from one generation to another, passing on valuable lessons. He watches over us closely, checking on our growth. Sometimes, like the third bud that disappeared, our plans don't come to fruition for reasons we don't understand. Sometimes He may need to prune the excess from our lives, cutting away things that distract us from paying attention to Him. Yet, in God's perfect time, He fulfills His purpose for each of our lives, allowing us to fully bloom.

Chapter 8

Getting to the Root of the Matter

Why do we have to have wisdom teeth anyway? I thought as Sarah and I left her appointment with the oral surgeon. She had witnessed her older brother's uncomfortable recovery after having his wisdom teeth removed several years before, so Sarah dreaded the inevitable ordeal.

Several weeks later on the day before her appointment of the scheduled surgery, Michael and I prayed with Sarah that the Lord would protect her from any harm. After the doctor removed her teeth and while she recovered from the sedative, he informed us that one of the impacted teeth was more difficult to extract than the others. "She's probably going to have a bit of pain after the Novacaine wears off," he said and gave her prescriptions for a strong pain medication along with a milder one.

When we returned home, Sarah followed the doctor's orders of applying ice packs and sipping on cool liquids. Our goal for the day consisted of making her as

Getting to the Root of the Matter

comfortable as possible. Michael and I were ready to treat Sarah like a queen. While she sat in the reclining chair with packages of frozen peas resting on her gauze-filled cheeks, she gazed at me with tired eyes. I wondered what agonizing discomfort would follow when the Novacaine wore off and earnestly wanted to speed up the recovery time in some way.

Sarah's weary expression prompted me to remember a prayer that had been taught during a healing conference we had attended months before. When the leader, a physician, had asked if anyone present was in pain at that moment, three people responded. The rest of us were encouraged to pray for these people repeating numerous times: "I rebuke this pain in Jesus' name." At the end of our prayer, the three people were questioned about their level of pain. All had received some relief.

After remembering this, I turned to Michael and exclaimed, "We should rebuke Sarah's pain in Jesus' name!" We both held her hands and began to pray, "We rebuke any pain in Jesus' name." Next, we rebuked the swelling, and lastly, we rebuked any abnormal bleeding.

When we finished praying this simple, but powerful prayer, Michael said, "It's as though repeating those words has strengthened my belief in what we prayed." I agreed. Through the next several days, we witnessed our daughter having minimal swelling, bleeding, and discomfort. She only needed a much smaller dose of the mild pain medicine than the doctor had ordered.

In the truest sense of showing empathy to Sarah's predicament, my husband had a toothache a couple of days prior to Sarah's tooth extractions. After a dental evaluation on Michael's ailing tooth, the dentist determined that the roots of the tooth were dying and recommended a root canal.

The words *root canal* conjured up thoughts in my mind of a painful experience. A few days later when Michael had the dental procedure, we believed that Jesus would be our Root and take care of the pain as He had for Sarah. We prayed again, "We rebuke the pain in Jesus' name."

Michael soon began eating a dinner of soft foods. Impatiently wanting to know if the Lord had heard our prayers, I asked Michael mid-way through the meal, "Does it hurt yet?"

"The Novacaine is starting to wear off, but it really doesn't hurt." He then added, "I think I'll be able to go to church tonight." An hour later, Michael drove off to a weekly Bible study. Although we shouldn't have been, we were amazed that he had very little discomfort throughout the evening meeting and even through the night and next day.

Through these experiences, the Lord has reminded us of His words, "Again, I tell you that if two of you on earth agree about anything you ask for, it will be done for you by my Father in heaven. For where two or three come together in my name, there am I with them."[1] By witnessing God's awesome ways, this promise is now rooted more firmly in our minds.

Chapter 9

Signs from the Great Matchmaker

"You won't believe this, but someone is going to buy my house!" Sally exclaimed at our divine appointment in a clothing store. "They plan to put a contract on it this afternoon!"

I had met Sally several years before in our Sunday school class. The glow on her face and the humble words in her prayers revealed her strong faith in the Lord. Since the time we first met, Sally has faced the challenges of breast cancer and later, a divorce. Our friendship has grown in recent years as we have enjoyed prayer times together and shared common interests.

For months I joined Sally in prayer, asking the Lord to send her a Christian companion. Many weeks later, she received an e-mail from someone on *Christian Mingle.com*. I was excited for Sally until she told me he lived miles away from Virginia in Washington State. But, in time, it became evident that the Lord was the Great Matchmaker for them.

Living in His Light

After daily e-mails, frequent phone calls, and a few trips across the country to see each other, Sally and Gary decided to marry. She began making arrangements to move out to Washington to spend a season of dating before entering marriage. A fully furnished room for her to rent in a house near Gary's home awaited her arrival.

Sally proceeded with plans to move and put her house on the market, even though it was a highly unfavorable time to sell her home. Several people viewed her home initially but made no offers. A month later, "For Sale" signs were planted in the yards of four more houses on her street. The houses that were similar to Sally's were priced less, increasing the competition. Although initially she had not wanted to rent out her home, she sensed it was wise to try.

The following day, Sally was amazed when she received a rental contract from a nice family. They even wanted to rent it for two years instead of one. "This is better than I could have imagined!" Sally rejoiced.

However, discouraging words came from the realtor later that week. "The family has had to back out of the contract because the sale of their house has fallen through."

Sally called Gary. "I have eighteen boxes all packed up—I've even taken everything off the walls!" They felt disappointed but wanted to trust God. After praying for answers to their dilemma, the house soon went back on the renter's market.

Several days later, the realtor contacted Sally. "You're not going to believe this, but the gentleman who looked at your house two days ago wants to buy it. He's a minister and feels the Lord has given him a sign through your license plate." The message displayed on Sally's license, "Luke 9:24," instructs us to follow God. "I'll be meeting with him this afternoon to write up a contract," the realtor added.

The Lord not only blessed Sally with a buyer for her house but also allowed in the contract the financial provisions she needed. He even provided the closing date on the day when her sons would leave for college, thus giving Sally the perfect time frame for moving. She had been praying for a confirmation from God that she should move. Clearly, this was it.

Sally packed her belongings, and Gary helped her move. Before they headed west, Gary gave Michael and me a shofar, a ram's horn. We graciously accepted his generous gift and didn't tell him we had just ordered one from a company in Israel. Michael and I decided we would simply return the new one to the company when it arrived.

A couple of weeks later on August 28th, our wedding anniversary, we received the package from Israel. Michael opened the box. As he pulled out the shofar, our eyes met. "Maybe we shouldn't return it but accept it as an anniversary gift from the Lord," I said.

"Definitely!" he said. We soon realized that I was able to blow the shofar that Gary had given us better than the new one. Michael could easily blow the new horn better than the other one. We are currently learning to blow them in tune together.

Sally and Gary are now happily married. Truly, the Lord is the Great Matchmaker in many ways along life's journey—in marriage, in friendships, and in the search for a home—and sometimes even with unexpected gifts, like shofars.

Chapter 10

Lifted Burdens

A soft lump had perched itself on Josh's shoulder for several years. He saw a doctor and learned that it was a lypoma, a benign fatty tumor. Later he scheduled an appointment with a plastic surgeon to have it removed.

Two days before the surgery, Josh told my husband, Michael, and me during a phone call that he had been unable to find a ride to the office, which was located twenty miles from his apartment in Ohio. Because he would receive an IV sedative for the surgery, he needed to plan for a ride home. I wondered if God wanted Josh to have this lump removed another time, and I asked him if he had prayed about it. Michael and I had not prayed about it either, so we all decided to pray fervently that the Lord would clearly reveal if he should have the surgery.

Josh called the following day with the news that he had cancelled the appointment. The Lord had led him to the Scripture in Psalm 81:6, "I removed the burden from their shoulders." We all sensed the Lord had a different plan.

Living in His Light

Several months later, Josh, Michael, and I attended a medical healing conference. We were blessed to hear testimonies of God's healing grace. On our ride home, I wondered if Josh's lypoma had decreased in size, according to the Lord's promise to remove the burden from his shoulder one day. When I asked him about it, he replied, "The lump doesn't bother me, but the sore muscles in my neck and shoulders bother me a lot!" Josh had been plagued with achy neck muscles sporadically for months, which he had blamed on practicing his violin or working at the computer for long periods of time.

The next week on a Tuesday afternoon, I felt a strong urge to go to the church sanctuary and pray for Josh. As I sat in a pew, I realized afresh that my son was truly flesh of my flesh and bone of my bone. This thought brought direction to my prayer prompting me to place my hand on my back. I prayed the Lord would touch Josh's back wherever it needed to be healed. At the exact time I prayed, the church clock rang three times. Immediately, I sensed the Lord had heard my prayers and had plans to remove the burden of pain from Josh's shoulders.

I shared this experience with Michael that evening and planned to write Josh a long e-mail the next morning. However, the following morning there was an e-mail from Josh that he had written the night before. He wrote, "Did you read what time Tuesday? Praise God!" Intrigued and perplexed by his question, I wrote back asking him to explain it. From Josh's response I learned that *What Time Tuesday?* is the name of a book he had received at the recent conference. He had read it the night before, only hours after I had been at the sanctuary. The book told about a specialized type of upper cervical chiropractic care called NUCCA (National Upper Cervical Chiropractic Association), which corrects any misalignment of the top bone of the spine called the *atlas*, where the head sits. When I talked to Josh later that day, he had already made an appointment with a doctor who practiced this method.

During Josh's first appointment, the doctor asked him numerous questions and took x-rays. After identifying the problem, he pressed firmly on the side of Josh's head behind his ear on the atlas bone, which corrected most of the alignment problem. The chiropractor informed him that it would take time for the muscles to conform to being in the proper positions, and he would need to return for a few follow-up visits for evaluation of that.

Josh quickly felt dramatic results from the procedure. On his way out of the office, he realized he could look up without feeling any resistance in his neck muscles—something he never knew was amiss. He also noticed that his legs were now even. Previously, one hip was higher than the other, causing a difference in how he walked and creating more tension in his back.

A few months after Josh's treatments, I began to have flare-ups of chronic shoulder and neck pain, which had surfaced occasionally through the years. There are only two NUCCA chiropractors in Virginia, and I soon located one in Charlottesville, only an hour away from our home.

At the first appointment, the doctor took x-rays and did other measurement tests, which determined that my atlas bone was out of alignment. Using the same technique Josh had received, the chiropractor adjusted the atlas bone to its correct position. From this painless, quick procedure without any loud popping noises, I gained immediate release of tension in my neck and free rotation of my head. Along with this freedom, I sensed a new ability to hold my shoulders up easily, something that had escaped me for a long time. Also, a fullness sensation that I had in one ear for years, though it had never exhibited any evidence of a tangible problem, greatly decreased.

Michael also opted to have this treatment, which has strengthened his back and greatly decreased the volume of his snoring, an unexpected blessing for me. We both wonder what future advantages we'll see from this treatment as the Lord brings us to better health through the expertise of this doctor's hands.

Sometimes we carry burdens without knowing what the real problem is, but I believe the Lord desires to remove those burdens. By looking to Him with trust, He enables us to answer affirmatively that familiar question, *Is your head on straight?*

Chapter 11

God Provides

Even when I may not understand the purpose of lingering suffering, I have learned that God reveals His continued care in the midst of those times. Today, the life expectancy for many people has lengthened as medical advancements have increased. For many families, extended lifetimes create opportunities to treasure more memories with loved ones. But sometimes, challenging health issues may prompt a roller coaster ride of ups and downs.

Recently my friend, Marcia, shared with me what happened when her 86-year-old father stepped onto his own roller coaster ride. During a phone call to her father, who lives 800 miles away from Marcia, something seemed wrong. "Dad, I can't understand what you're saying—your words aren't clear." After telling him "good-bye," she immediately called her brother, a physician. He called the nurse at the senior citizen facility where their dad lives. In

Living in His Light

minutes, an ambulance arrived to transport their father to the nearby hospital. Tests and x-rays indicated pneumonia.

The next day, Marcia and her husband George traveled to be with her father. His health gradually improved, but after seventeen days in the hospital, he remained weak. His doctor advised him to move to a rehabilitation facility for several weeks before returning home. Since none of his three children lived close to him, Marcia and her brothers would not be able to visit their father regularly. Therefore, finding an excellent rehabilitation center became a priority.

The case manager at the hospital assisted by giving Marcia a list of places to evaluate. While looking over the list, Marcia noticed there were three facilities in a town where her father grew up—only an hour away. His sister and several cousins lived near this town, as did some of his friends from high school. One of the three choices of rehab centers clearly seemed to be the right one: a calm, orderly environment in a beautiful building. Marcia sensed her dad would feel right at home there since the director of nurses was one of his cousins. Although this seemed to be the perfect place, no rooms were available.

When Marcia and George visited her dad at the hospital the next day, they learned, much to their surprise, that he would be discharged that day. They felt mounting distress about this predicament. Minutes later, the pastor came to visit, and Marcia asked for prayer about the urgent situation. Shortly after they prayed, the case manager came by the room and said, "The rehab center you wanted

God Provides

just called. They have a room available!" She then added, "If you get the paperwork to the facility by 2 p.m., your dad can have the room." Marcia and George were elated!

They began discussing how they could get in touch with the physician who would need to fill out the transfer papers. Moments later, her dad's doctor stopped by the room. Marcia explained their dilemma. Great peace came over her as she listened to the doctor's response, "I can have that paperwork done in fifteen minutes!"

That afternoon her dad was transported to the rehab center. When entering his new room, he announced, "Well, I feel like I have just checked into the Hilton!"

They were in awe of the mighty ways the Lord had provided the best place for her father to recover. Although initially Marcia had hoped he would be in a facility near the town he had resided in recent years, she now realized that God had the best plan. By returning to his hometown, he has renewed friendships with old high school friends, as well as nearby relatives. Visitors stop by to see him every day. And when it's time to leave the rehab center, Marcia knows, without a doubt, the Lord will provide the next place for her dad to move and call *home.*

Chapter 12

Memory of Hope

In the summer of 2005, we planned a special birthday party for our daughter, Sarah, just before she left for college. Her birthday is August twenty-first. From the time she was little and first learned about days on a calendar, Sarah has enjoyed reminding us of the significance of the twenty-first day in each passing month. We often laughed about it, and in our household she became known as the "birthday girl."

Mixed emotions filled my mind, as I knew this upcoming season of life would cause significant changes for our family. Michael and I would be empty nesters, and Sarah would start a new chapter of independence. For a few minutes I became lost in my memories of previous birthday celebrations, as well as the days long ago when I had prepared to go to college. My thoughts drifted to the time when one of my dad's hunting dogs had given birth to frail puppies. Dad always looked for strong dogs with

Memory of Hope

each new litter. But this time only two puppies were born, and one had already died.

"This puppy will probably die, too," Dad said, shrugging. "They're just weaklings." I hardly could bear that thought.

"Could we at least let Fido sleep in the utility room instead of the doghouse?" I asked. After my parents agreed to allow that, Mom and I fixed a cozy spot with some old towels. I brought the puppy inside, gently laying him on the soft bed we made. I placed a small bowl of water beside him, hoping he would drink. Feeling helpless, I called my friend Mary.

"Have you thought about praying for him?" she asked.

"Not really. Fido is just a puppy," I reminded her.

"It can't hurt to pray, can it?"

"I guess not," I said.

After our conversation, I petted Fido and prayed for him, then left him alone as he slept. Later that afternoon while I finished packing to leave home for college the next day, my friend Kay stopped by. I shared with her about our sick puppy. As we continued to talk, my mother came to my room. Smiling from ear to ear, she announced, "You won't believe this, but that puppy is starting to wiggle around and even raised his head to sip some water!" Kay and I looked at each other and laughed. My simple heartfelt prayer had been heard!

The puppy grew stronger in the days ahead. Later that year when I arrived home from school for a weekend visit, Fido came running up to me. My dad called across the yard, "You know, Fido is one of the best hunting dogs I've ever had."

Now many years later, as we helped Sarah pack for college, I thought, *If the Lord had healed my puppy, wouldn't He surely heal Sarah?* She had been in remission of Crohn's disease for two years, but I wondered what challenges she would face in the college environment. I felt grateful that Sarah was healthy enough to embark on this new adventure. However, prior to leaving home, her doctor wanted Sarah to have a CT scan done to ensure there weren't any hidden problems.

On August twenty-fourth, the day of the scheduled CT scan, tears filled my eyes even before I crawled out of bed. I felt sad Sarah had to deal with this. I just wanted her to have a special week before going to college. It didn't seem fair. I definitely wanted a confirmation that all would be well.

Then I remembered I had written about the puppy in my diary. I ran to find the box that contained my old journals. My mind was filled with emotion as I wondered what the Lord might reveal to me. Could it be that the puppy was healed on this very same date, August twenty-fourth?

When I opened the box, I soon found the old diary. With excitement I thumbed through the month of August. I turned to the page for August twenty-fourth, and my heart sank when I read of my day's events at nursing school.

Although disappointed, curiosity prompted me to flip through previous pages, and when I found the page about the puppy, the tears began to fall again. This time they were tears of joy as I read the date--August twenty-first! For Sarah, the "birthday girl," August twenty-first was the most special date in her life! What a perfect way to receive a clear confirmation of God's healing promise.

The CT scan report showed a small area of thickening in the intestinal wall, but it was not an obvious problem. Further testing was suggested and scheduled four months later during Sarah's Christmas break from college. Somehow I sensed God had already revealed to us what the results would be...normal! Three years before, I had hung onto the words "just believe." Through His awesome ways, I finally believed.

*The book *Reaching for Answers to Crohn's Disease* describes Sarah's journey to restored health from Crohn's disease. She remains well by the grace of God and by simply following a restricted sugar diet and taking the probiotic Culturelle®.

Chapter 13

What Happens When I Go Home?

"The itching keeps getting worse," my mother-in-law, Sylvia, said to my husband, Michael, during a phone call. After a visit with her doctor, she began using cream that he had prescribed. But the itching failed to improve, so two weeks later she returned for a follow-up appointment.

"I think we have a bigger problem than the itching," her doctor gently informed her as he noticed the jaundice color of her skin. He ordered a CT scan and MRI. Since the results of the MRI indicated liver changes, the doctor admitted Sylvia to the hospital for further tests.

Michael and I had wanted to talk to Sylvia about Jesus ever since Michael became a Christian twenty-five years before. However, Sylvia did not want to discuss that topic, so we never did. Gradually in recent years, Michael ended his weekly phone calls with her saying, "I love you, and God loves you, too." He began to encourage her to read

What Happens When I Go Home?

Scripture from her Hebrew Bible, and it became easier to talk to her about God.

From the results of the additional medical tests, we sensed Sylvia's time on earth was limited to weeks. Her health deteriorated quickly after the first days of her hospital stay, and our prayers for her became more fervent. We asked others to join us in praying that the Lord would reveal Himself to her in a way that we couldn't. Michael assured his mother of our refuge in God: "My soul finds rest in God alone; my salvation comes from him. He alone is my rock and my salvation; He is my fortress, I will never be shaken."[1]

In Sylvia's hospital room, a white-board hung that listed numerous questions and information. We were intrigued with the question: "What happens when I go home?"

Each time we visited Sylvia, she responded to our voices with sighs. Our son and daughter, Josh and Sarah, lived far away from their grandmother's home in Virginia Beach, Virginia. They weren't able to visit their grandmother at that time, but they called. While Michael held the phone close to his mother's ear, Josh and Sarah said prayers for her. Sarah played her banjo and sang praise songs. Josh played Hebrew songs on his violin. During these phone calls, Michael and I watched Sylvia's expressions. Sometimes her utterances changed pitch, seemingly indicating she enjoyed their music and words.

Although Sylvia's doctor predicted she would not make it through the weekend, her condition remained the same four days later. On the following Monday morning, Michael and I perceived we should talk to Sylvia about forgiveness. We wondered if there was something we needed to say or that she desired to say but could not.

When we arrived at the hospital that morning, I located Sylvia's nurse to ask, "If it's okay, my husband and I would like to have some uninterrupted time with Sylvia to pray with her."

"Sure," she said and then inquired, "What religion are you?" I suspected she was confused, since she knew Sylvia was Jewish but saw that I wore a cross necklace.

"Michael and I are Christians, and we've been reading Scriptures to Sylvia and praying for the past several days," I explained.

Her eyes welled up with tears. "Oh, you're going to make me cry," she said. We both shed tears. "Would you like for me to put a sign on the door saying 'No Visitors?'" she asked.

"That would be great!"

She walked to the nurses' station to get paper as I walked toward Sylvia's room, but before I opened the door, I called to the nurse. "By the way, what is your name?"

She turned around and smiled. "Faith," she said.

I laughed. "Of course!"

While Michael and I held Sylvia's hands, we asked for forgiveness for anything we may have done to hurt her. We told her that if there was anything she wanted to forgive us about, we understood.

What Happens When I Go Home?

"Mom," Michael said, "just like Isaiah prophesized in the Old Testament Scriptures, Yeshua, (Hebrew name for Jesus) came to take away our sins. He died on the cross to become our Savior...and your Savior, too." Michael explained further. "All you need to do, Mom, is to accept Him in your heart."

In the quiet time that followed, I looked down at the bracelet I was wearing that had Scripture engraved on it. "Now, faith is being sure of what we hope for and certain of what we do not see."[2] As I reread it out loud, the word "faith" grabbed our attention. The Lord had even given Sylvia a special nurse named Faith, affirming His care for us all.

Before leaving that night to head home for a time of rest, we kissed her and said "good-bye." Michael told her that perhaps she could go home, too, into the arms of Yeshua.

At 3:30 a.m. the next morning, we received a phone call that Sylvia had passed away. I realized at that moment that we had only paid attention to the word *faith* on my bracelet. But now *all* of the words in that Scripture from Hebrews 11:1 were being impressed upon me: "Now, faith is being sure of what we hope for and certain of what we do not see."

When Michael and I sat in Sylvia's room the day before, we were looking for an obvious sign, something big, indicating that the Lord had revealed Himself to her. Instead, He had quietly provided us with His powerful words on my bracelet, giving us a clear, profound message.

Living in His Light

He reminded us that sometimes we are too busy looking for a sign *we want to see*, thus we often miss the message He places directly in front of us. Michael and I realized that in the Lord's awesome ways He provided us with *hope* for the *unseen*. We may not know until we get to heaven how the Lord revealed Himself to Sylvia, but one thing we sense, for certain, is that He did.

Chapter 14

The Salute

It was a beautiful summer evening on the shores of southern Virginia. My husband, our daughter, Sarah, and I had made the trip to the beach with a specific purpose.

"Let's head down that way," Michael said, pointing to the more isolated area of the beach. We walked along the shore looking for the perfect location to have a prayer as I carried the container of ashes. My Uncle Dan had chosen to be cremated and did not want a memorial service. With most of his family already gone and friends no longer nearby, he didn't want to worry anyone with extra plans.

We had come to the beach later in the evening hoping to have privacy for this occasion. While we waited for the lingering fishermen to gather their gear and leave, I thought about Uncle Dan and his life.

He was born in 1925, two years after my mother. He loved to sail and had even built a small sailboat after taking a woodworking class in high school. His love for

Living in His Light

the sea prompted his enlistment in the Navy in the 1940s. Uncle Dan had hoped he would be assigned to a ship and travel far, but the Navy had others plans for his bright mind. They sent him to the University of Colorado where he received an engineering degree. He never did receive an assignment in the Navy to travel out to sea, but he later traveled all over the world as an engineer designing pump systems.

Uncle Dan lived miles away from us, so we didn't see him often. When I was a child, he visited our family every Christmas, and each summer we traveled to Upper Montclair, New Jersey, to see him. Since he lived near New York City, he took us to see the sights during our visits. He often extended his generosity to us and to others. At the age of 72, he received an award from the Red Cross for donating 192 pints of blood in his lifetime.

On June 6th, 2011, his stepdaughter called me with the message that Uncle Dan had passed away that morning. She asked if I wanted any of his ashes. I accepted her offer, knowing that I wanted to recognize and honor this special uncle. When I received the ashes, I thought about the ways Uncle Dan had touched my life and the lives of others. I knew that one of his greatest desires when he was young was to go out to sea. The Atlantic Ocean seemed like a perfect place for his remains to rest.

When the fishermen left the quiet beach, we walked to the shoreline with the ashes, ready to say "good-bye" to Uncle Dan. The sun's reflection spanned across the ocean. While we stood at the edge of the shore, we had a time

The Salute

of prayer. Each of us took a handful of ashes and tossed them into the rippling waves. The gentle breeze carried them further into the vast waters.

"Look above us!" Michael exclaimed. A flock of pelicans in a v-shape formation flew over us. My Uncle Dan was now receiving an honorable salute—one he greatly deserved. Although he had not wanted any special recognition, other plans obviously had been orchestrated by the One over the highest ranks.

As we watched the pelicans fly toward the sunset, keeping their formation, we sauntered away from the shore. We gazed at the sun drift beyond the horizon. Without a doubt, we knew that Uncle Dan was now home—and in the presence of his Commander.

Chapter 15

A Mother's Journey Home

"**O**h, Lord, this is too big!" I cried. "Where are You?"

I had just received a call from my mother's doctor, who informed me that her chest x-ray looked suspicious. A week before, an ultrasound had revealed a pelvic mass. Tests were scheduled to confirm a diagnosis of ovarian cancer. The doctor was kind in answering my questions. I sensed he genuinely cared about my mother's health as he tried to ease the harsh news of possible metastases. He reminded me that I had been blessed with my 81-year-old mother for many years. I knew I needed to realize the number of years ahead was limited.

Nonetheless, when I hung up the phone, the tears began to flow. My faith in God's healing power had grown in recent years as I had seen His hand move in amazing ways, but at that moment, my hope for Mom's restored health disappeared. I felt bitterness that the Lord would take her home this way. Even though her years were many,

A Mother's Journey Home

she had continued to be His useful servant, filling in as organist in her church whenever needed and giving generously to her family and others. Her kindness and selflessness reached all those she met, and her faith in God ran deep. It didn't seem fair for her to receive this devastating diagnosis.

I asked the Lord to grant me comfort and understanding in some way. When I picked up my Bible, the pages fell open to the story about Hezekiah's illness, and I began to read. Hezekiah had prayed, "'Remember, O LORD, how I have walked before you faithfully and with wholehearted devotion and have done what is good in your eyes.' And Hezekiah wept bitterly."[1]

These words grabbed my attention since minutes before I had been describing to the Lord similar characteristics about my mother. I too wept bitterly. I read further. The Lord said, "I have heard your prayer and seen your tears; I will heal you."[2]

This Scripture brought hope to me that the Lord would lengthen Mom's life. It was time to watch how the Conductor would direct His baton for music to flow from my mother's fingers and for her song of kindness to continue to reach others. I tried to hold onto this profound message in the days ahead, but as the challenges of dealing with Mom's illness mounted, doubts surfaced.

Surgery was scheduled. When my brothers and I stood at Mom's stretcher before she was taken to the operating room, the anesthesiologist asked if we were aware of my mother's heart murmur. Normally, it had not caused her any problems, but this doctor informed us of the high stress that surgery would place on her heart. Nevertheless, we all felt it was imperative to follow through with surgery because the cancer was causing her discomfort and spreading quickly.

The time arrived for my brothers and me to say "goodbye" to Mom before they rolled her to the operating room. I gave her a hug. "Jesus is watching over you," I said in a loud voice since she had impaired hearing. As I walked away, I thought of the Lord's sense of humor. He had prompted me to speak those words loudly, enabling them to be heard by my mother and also to reach the ears of the medical staff, as well as other patients and families in the waiting area.

When we met with the doctor after the operation, he reported that he had removed four large tumors. No problems occurred with her heart! Through the following weeks, Mom gradually recovered from surgery. Chemotherapy treatments followed. The oncologist informed us that the chemotherapy would only prevent the cancer lesions in her lungs from getting bigger. He stated it would not reduce the number of lesions or shrink them.

While she went through the treatments, Mom moved to an assisted living facility. Her white blood cell and platelet counts dipped below normal sometimes, but even with frail health, her positive attitude always shone through.

At the end of the course of seven chemotherapy treatments, lab work indicated that the drugs had worked, slowing the progression of the cancer. Time would tell how long it would last, but my mother opted not to have future treatments to combat it. Following her last treatment, Mom moved to a different assisted living apartment permanently, since living alone at home was not wise due to her declining health. She adjusted well to her new home. Using a walker to get around, she named it *Ruth,* referencing the Scripture, "...for whither thou goest, I will go."[3] She sewed for others, played the piano, and kept up with other resident's birthdays making sure they received a card signed by their neighbors. She soon became an inspiration to many with her persistent positive outlook on life, and it was evident the Lord had extended her days to be His faithful servant.

The Concert

Since Mom decided against having any further chemotherapy treatments, her family doctor chose not to order tests to monitor the cancer. The plan was to treat her symptomatically. Two years after she had received the cancer diagnosis, she complained of one side of her rib cage feeling sore. The doctor ordered a chest x-ray to determine the pain's origin. He thought the cancer may have spread to her bones, but the x-ray indicated a tiny fracture on each of two ribs. The fractures were possibly linked with osteoporosis and caused by Mom pulling clothes out of the washing machine.

The x-ray also provided a perfect opportunity to note whether the cancer lesions in her lungs had changed. As the doctor shared the results of the radiology report, I listened in amazement. There were fewer lesions! We all remembered the oncologist's words explaining this would not happen.

After another year, a chest x-ray indicated that Mom's lungs were cancer free! However, a few months later, she felt a hard mass in her abdomen. I wondered if the season of her healing on earth was over. But the Lord continued to nudge me to pray for my mother's healing even though the circumstances revealed reasons to doubt.

During one of her hospitalizations due to back pain and dehydration, I witnessed remarkable ways the Lord revealed Himself. Mom's condition appeared to be deteriorating quickly after several days in the hospital, with edema increasing in her legs and arms. My sister-in-law, Sandy, called late one afternoon. "I think you should come. Your mother is having more difficulty breathing."

My husband and I quickly packed our suitcase and started out on the two-hour trip from Richmond to Franklin, Virginia. Our son, Josh, had been in North Carolina visiting friends and was traveling back to Richmond at that time. When I called him inquiring about meeting us in Franklin, I learned that he had just entered Virginia and was not far from a major intersection leading straight to Franklin.

By the time we arrived at the hospital to meet Josh and other family members, Mom was feeling much better.

Josh mentioned that he had been to a music store while he was in North Carolina and had bought a banjo for our daughter, since she was learning to play. She was not able to be there that night, but my older brother was, who also plays the banjo. Soon, we listened to a beautiful concert that evening performed by Josh, playing his violin, and my brother, playing the banjo.

Two hours before, when we were driving to Franklin, we wondered what the night would bring. I now knew this was the reason the Lord had guided us all together. While I watched my mother sitting in the reclining chair with her feet propped up thoroughly enjoying the company and the music, I realized that only God could have orchestrated that special visit and concert.

Sweet Potato Lesson

Due to continued back pain and adverse reactions to medicines, my mother's hospitalization turned into weeks. I felt frustrated that I couldn't be there to help her more, but distance between our homes hindered that. I made frequent phone calls to check on Mom and spent much time praying about the challenges that arose for her. Nevertheless, I used a lot of energy worrying about details that I could not control.

When I visited her, I thought of tasks I could do to provide more comfort. Since her appetite and ability to chew had diminished greatly leading to a soft diet, I shopped for foods and prepared things that she might like.

I remembered she had not been served sweet potatoes during her hospital stay. One morning I whipped up a sweet potato casserole and felt proud of myself for coming up with that idea. Surely it would be a nice diversion from the usual ground up food she received. When I arrived at her hospital room minutes before lunch, a dining service worker brought her the meal tray. I lifted the lid expecting to see the choices of food that had been sent before, but instead, whipped sweet potatoes filled half of the plate. They even looked much tastier than the ones I had made, so I placed mine in the refrigerator for another time.

My mother ate more than she had for a few days. I couldn't help but smile as I thought of the Scripture, "'Martha, Martha,' the Lord answered, 'you are worried and upset about many things, but only one thing is needed.'"[4]

Many times I overload my day trying to accomplish more than I can handle. My thoughts often focus on the troubles instead of the Problem Solver. But through this experience, the Lord clearly reminded me that all I need to do is keep my eyes on Him and trust that He will take care of details in ways that I can't even imagine. He also reminded me that He frequently uses someone else to provide the solution. I often remember the day I learned the sweet potato lesson. And sometimes, when I race ahead of God, I hear His voice saying "Martha, Martha..."

Clearing the Confusion

My mother's hospital stay continued into a third week. Her back pain greatly diminished, and she became progressively stronger. However, late one night I received an e-mail from my brother John, who lives near Mom. He reported she had seemed a little confused that day. She had not received any pain medicine in the previous few days, so I perceived that wouldn't be the cause. Nevertheless, I recalled that she was on a medication to stimulate her appetite. It seemed appropriate for her to take this medicine, but now I wondered if it was causing her confusion.

I promptly looked up information about this drug and learned that possible adverse reactions included confusion and abnormal thinking, and also edema. I quickly called the nurses' station and requested that they withhold the medicine until we could talk to the doctor.

The next day, during a phone call with my brother, I learned that Mom's confusion was much worse. Hallucinations puzzled her mind all day. The doctor had discontinued the appetite stimulant, and time would tell if it was the culprit. Later that day before I called John who was at my mother's room, I asked the Lord for an encouraging sign that this confusion would pass. When I talked to my brother, I could hear Mom in the background uttering incoherent phrases. Previously, she had been sharp-minded, avidly reading much of the time and keeping up with current events. This confused behavior was not like her at all and concerned me greatly.

"Do you want to talk to Martha, your daughter?" John asked her.

He handed Mom the phone, and she asked, "Are you still planning to come on Saturday?"

"Yes, we are—that's tomorrow, and we'll be there."

Then, she mentioned that John and his wife, Sandy, had been with her most of the day, which they had. She returned the phone to my brother.

"Those were the most cognizant words she has said all day!" he announced. To me, her ability to say those words revealed an answer to prayer.

While my husband and I were driving to Franklin the next day to visit her, John called to forewarn us about Mom's condition. She had tried to get out of the bed a few times the night before and remained confused at breakfast time. I wondered how I was going to handle seeing her in this state. If the medicine was the cause, it had taken over a week to build up in her system, and I assumed it might take awhile for normal thinking to resume.

Arriving at the hospital, we held onto the hope that she would know us. We slowly opened the door to her room. She was lying on her side facing away from us with her eyes closed. When I touched her shoulder, she opened her eyes. "I am so very glad to see you," I said with a lump in my throat.

With a big grin and frail voice, she replied, "I am so glad to see you, too!" We hugged each other tightly.

"Do you know where you are, Mom?"

"Yes, I'm in the hospital."

I began asking her other questions, which she answered appropriately. Michael and I looked at each other with tears welling up in both of us.

Mom began telling us about the strange experiences she had had in the past day, stating that it all seemed so real but confusing to her. However, it was now evident she no longer was confused. Throughout the day, the edema began subsiding, too. Truly, the Great Physician made a house call to my mother that day! And we were exceedingly grateful.

Just Rejoice

"The emergency room doctor says your mother is probably not going to make it through the night," Sandy said when she called late one afternoon. A week before, Mom was discharged from the hospital and had returned to her assisted living apartment. She had improved in the previous days and even celebrated her 86th birthday, but her health was now deteriorating quickly. Nurses from the hospice health care services were helping her feel more comfortable. However, she began struggling to breathe, thus, she was transported to the emergency room, where a chest x-ray revealed a large mass in her lungs. It seemed that the cancer was aggressively attacking her body. I had been praying for my mother's release from suffering for months, and now, along with deep sadness, I experienced a sense of pending relief for her.

A day earlier I had mailed a letter to Mom describing the many ways she had positively impacted my life. Although I had mentioned some of these things previously to her, I felt the need to articulate the words more clearly in a letter. Since she had left her apartment before the mail came, I now feared she would never read it. I remembered I had made a copy of the letter to keep. During our phone call, I asked if it was possible for her to listen to me read it. Through tears, I read the letter. With her frail voice and labored breathing, she expressed her appreciation for the endearing words.

"Now don't you fret," she added. "I'm going to another world, and it's going to be great. Just rejoice!"

"Oh, Mom, I know, and you won't have to suffer anymore."

"That's right!"

With renewed composure I continued, "I just want you to know that we are going to have a special celebration of your life. Josh is going to play his violin as we've talked about before, and as you've requested, we'll have Bach music. I love you so very much, Mom."

"I love you, too," she said.

"Mike and I are getting ready to come be with you, so we'll see you soon."

"Okay. Bye now."

"Bye-bye." I hung up the phone and sobbed. I had felt the joy of knowing the Lord many times and had a strong belief in His promise of eternal life, but it still hurt deeply to say "good-bye" to my mother.

My mother chose to return to her apartment room to sleep peacefully in her own bed rather than in the hospital. When we arrived at her room later that evening, John, Sandy, and my younger brother David were there along with a nurse. Mom was lying on her side and appeared to be sleeping comfortably with her favorite soft pillows cushioning her. Soon she awoke, and we greeted her with hugs. She was able to speak clearly for short intervals of time for her breathing had improved with the aid of the oxygen machine. I sat in a chair beside her bed. As she continued to doze, I noticed her fingers. They knew the piano keys well and had brought the gift of music to many; now they were gently clasped together.

Michael and I remained with her until late in the night and then left to get some sleep. One of my brothers and a nurse kept vigil with Mom through the night. When Michael and I walked down the hall after leaving her room, the tears kept falling, but in my heart, I knew the words Mom had spoken earlier that evening were right—that where she was going would be great!

The Encore

After a night of sporadic sleeping, I awoke to the music of birds singing. Michael and I began the day praying for strength for the hours ahead. When I went to my mother's dimly lit room early that morning, I slowly walked to her bed. Mom opened her eyes and spoke clearly to me.

I sat beside her bed holding her hand while she dozed. She awoke and asked for some ice chips. With a spoon I placed some in her mouth...then she dozed. The next time she awoke, she asked for a sip of water...then rested again. A little while later, she asked if she could get up to the bathroom! With the help of the nurse and me and "Ruth," she walked steadily. While she was up, the nurse gave her a morning bath, and we noticed a large firm mass on the right side of my mother's back. Neither of us had noted that before, but it seemed that lumps had now planted themselves throughout her body. Firm masses could be felt at her abdomen, and yet my mother's body continued to fight this invasion.

I had expected Mom's condition to deteriorate through the night before but began to wonder if the Lord had other plans when she asked, "Can I sit up in the chair and read the newspaper?"

"Sure!" the nurse answered. Stunned, I watched my mother walk to her favorite chair. She sat down and reached for the newspaper. I could hardly wait to tell Pam, the nurse in charge.

"Maybe you should ask Pam to come down to your mother's room and see for herself," my mother's nurse said.

"That's a great idea!" We both laughed. I hurried down the hall to find her. "Pam, could you come to my mother's room?" I asked somberly.

"Do I need to bring anything?" she asked.

"No, just your eyes," I said, trying not to give away the surprise she was about to witness. When we reached my mother's room, I opened the door and watched with laughter the smile spread over Pam's face. She too gazed in awe at my mother nonchalantly reading the paper.

I phoned my brothers with words of utter amazement. Mom began to drink more and felt strong enough to visit us all throughout the day. In the weeks ahead, she began walking down the hall with "Ruth" to visit friends. She started new sewing projects and resumed writing letters to others encouraging them.

The Lord taught me that day that He can change all things, even when the wisdom from the medical community and visual evidence totally contradict His plans. During that encore of my mother's life song, I watched the Great Conductor continue directing the rhythm of my mother's days.

Preparing for a Heavenly Christmas

Almost six months had passed since Mom began receiving hospice care. Much to everyone's surprise, she had improved during that time. When our family visited her at Thanksgiving, she expressed disappointment that the six-month timeframe for receiving hospice care would soon be ending in December. The caretakers were special to her; the nurse and social worker had taken music lessons from my mother when she taught years before. She was pleased to become reacquainted with them and enjoyed their conversations. However, due to Mom's continual improvement, the hospice staff could not justify their continuing care for her.

I had looked forward to enjoying another Christmas with Mom. Unfortunately, three days after Thanksgiving, she had been rushed to the emergency room. Thoughts of spending Christmas with her quickly faded as I watched her struggle to simply breathe. Along with cancer, she now battled pneumonia.

Only a few days before going to the hospital, she had written a rough draft of her traditional Christmas letter to friends. She had worked hard at writing the letter, including the latest news about family members. I offered to type it and make copies for her as I had done in previous years.

Now, as she lay in the hospital bed, she realized the letter would need to be changed. "I can't do it," Mom said with her weak voice.

I then offered, "If it would be okay with you, I could add a note with the letter describing the current situation." She agreed to let me.

Mom had kept in touch with some of these friends for over 50 years, and I perceived this would also be an opportunity to ask for their prayers for her. This task became a priority since I knew how much Mom treasured keeping in touch with her friends. Neglecting other Christmas traditions no longer mattered to me. Many Christmas decorations remained in the attic, and I placed my usual baking on hold. Even though it seemed that she might not spend Christmas with us, I hung onto the hope that the Lord would provide special memories.

In between difficult moments of breathing, Mom managed to ask me, "Could you find the hymnal the next time you go to the apartment and bring it to me?"

"Sure," I said.

"I keep trying to remember how the third verse begins in *Away in a Manger,* and I want to see it." Years before, as our church's organist, she had taught the children's choir all three verses of *Away in a Manger.* The song had been going through her mind sporadically throughout the day, but some of the words in the third verse escaped her memory.

Later when I brought the hymnal to the hospital, she asked me to read the verses to her. I pulled my chair close to the bed in the dimly lit room and began reading the familiar words. Keeping my composure became more difficult as I read the third verse..."Be near me, Lord Jesus, I ask thee to stay close by me forever and love me, I pray. Bless all the dear children in thy tender care and fit us for heaven to live with thee there." Without my mother's awareness of my tears, she asked if I would read the hymn again. With a stumbling voice, I managed to read it once more. When I finished, Mom closed her eyes and peacefully drifted off to sleep.

In the following days, her breathing improved. Her strength gradually grew, and the physical therapy staff soon evaluated her for increased activity. A couple of days later the therapist brought a small piano keyboard to

Mom's room and asked her to play some Christmas carols. The music traveled down the hall, and before long others were gathering at her door.

Soon, Mom started receiving Christmas cards and letters from friends containing meaningful notes and expressions of prayer that brightened her days. Three days before Christmas, her doctor discharged her from the hospital. Even though she was strong enough to go back to her apartment, her health was still frail, which allowed the hospice staff to readmit her to their services. Mom was delighted!

On Christmas Eve, Mom slipped and fell to her knees, but did not break any bones. When I visited her later that day and asked her about it, she replied, "Well, after all, this is the season to 'fall on your knees.'" I couldn't help but laugh as I remembered my dad frequently singing those same words years before from one of his favorite songs, "O Holy Night."

At dinner on Christmas day, our family gathered together at Mom's apartment for a time of celebration. For the previous month I had watched the Lord bless my mother, His child, with His tender care...strengthening her and continuing to fit her for heaven. I realized that He had prepared my heart for Christmas in much greater ways than ever before. He instilled in my mind that in future Christmases, falling on my knees to give Him praise and opening my heart to Him and others will be the only preparations I will ever need.

Comforting Roses

As the months passed, Mom grew weary of the daily trials of life. Increased edema in her legs robbed her of independence. Limited mobility brought much frustration. With her frailty increasing, she couldn't wait to get that new body God promises. During one of my visits to my then 87 year-old-mother, she admitted to me, "I wonder when I'll be called home." And then she added, "I'm going to be on the lookout for it."

In the writings of C. S. Lewis, he described a yearning for heaven that perhaps now applied to my mother. "If I find in myself a desire which no experience in this world can satisfy, the most probable explanation is that I was made for another world."[5]

Several days after Mom announced her anticipation to be called home, I awoke with a strong yearning to search Scripture passages about God's glory. I had witnessed the Lord sustaining my mother through many health crises, and I wanted to know how to pray for her now. With a sharp mind and persistent positive attitude, she inspired many. I wondered if the Lord would extend her time on earth, allowing her to continue encouraging others. In my earnest prayer, I simply wanted Mom to be spared of further suffering.

After reading numerous Bible verses that morning and having prayer time, I turned on the computer and read the devotional I receive every day from the *Kenny Davis Ministries*. The Scripture spoke loud and clear to me: "This sickness will not end in death. No, it is for God's glory, so that God's son may be glorified."[6]

About an hour later, my brother called to report that Mom wasn't doing well that day and had slept most of the morning. After his call, I thought more about the devotional I had read earlier. I wondered if God was going to heal my mother on earth, or was He going to take her home?

That afternoon I talked to Mom briefly on the phone. She remained clear-minded. She was not in pain, and, in fact, had not taken any strong pain medicines for several months. We ended the call telling each other "I love you."

The following day, Mom became unresponsive. My husband and I packed our bags and headed to Franklin to be with her. Other family members were there when we arrived. By mid-afternoon they left for home since we perceived our mother might remain in this state for a long time. We had all said "good-bye" to Mom several times during the past year when it seemed the Lord was ready to take her, but then amazingly He didn't.

Michael and I remained with her during the afternoon. The sun was shining brightly through her window. While tears streamed down my face, I continued to hold her hand while I poured out my heart. "Mom, I'm going to miss you greatly, but I don't want you to suffer anymore. Surely we're going to see each other again one day. I love you so very much."

Although my mother made no verbal responses, I noticed tears from her eyes and gently wiped them along with my own. I looked around the room at her things—pictures of family members, her devotional book and Bible on the nearby table. Several little pillows she had made for extra comfort lay beside her. And then I looked at the cross-stitch picture with birds and Scripture from Psalm 84 she had sewn years ago. "Mom, I'm looking at the picture hanging over your bed, and I want to read the words. 'How lovely is your temple, O Lord...even the sparrows and swallows are welcome to come and rest among your altars. How happy are those who can live in your temple singing your praises.'"[7]

Only a few minutes after I read the last line, Mom took her last breath. Prior to this day, I feared I would not be able to bear witnessing the loss of my mother. I thought the pain would be more than my heart could endure. But instead, peace surrounded me as she appeared to simply fall asleep. And I believe, as Jesus promised, Mom's sickness did not end in death. Her body was only a vessel that housed her soul to fulfill God's purpose here on earth. I sensed she was now awakening to a new life in heaven for eternity.

Several days later, we had a beautiful service to honor my mother. It was a gloriously sunny day with only a slight winter chill in the air. The sun's rays filtered through the beautiful stained-glass windows of the church. Our son played his violin as his grandmother had requested—Bach music. My mother had been the organist at the church years before, so the rector knew her well. He shared touching stories about her that brought memories alive.

Living in His Light

Our daughter spoke about her grandmother with endearing words. She shared the words she had written in her Bible: "Let us not become weary in doing good, for at the proper time we will reap a harvest if we do not give up."[8] Mom had lived out this example.

Truly, as Sarah concluded in her words about her grandmother—my mother, "God revealed His glory in her life and body and now has called her home."

Although saying "good bye" to Mom was extremely difficult for me, I learned first-hand the Lord has amazing ways to give us comfort and heal our broken hearts. I continue to be in awe of the way He did that two weeks after my mother went to heaven.

It was a rainy day. I was driving home from a weekly Bible study. While the windshield wipers clattered across the window of my car, sweet memories of Mom crossed my mind. I too needed wipers for the tears falling down my face. I yearned for the Lord to console my grieving heart.

A few minutes after I arrived home, the phone rang. It was my friend, Rose. She told me she'd had a dream about my mother the night before and wanted to share it with me. I listened closely to her words. "You and your mother were sitting outside on the front porch at her assisted-living home. She turned to you and asked if you would finish sewing the Christmas tree comforter that had roses on it."

Mom loved to sew and had spent many of her last days working on quilt blocks, but none of them fit the

A Mother's Journey Home

description. However, the timing of Rose's call about her dream brought me much comfort. I thanked her for calling and added, "If I ever see any fabric with roses and Christmas trees, I will certainly purchase some and make a quilt!"

But I am learning the Lord always wants to bless us more than we expect. The following week I traveled to my mother's house to sort through her belongings. As I looked through the linen closet, I saw the Christmas quilt she made years ago. It had covered her bed during many past Christmas seasons. Although I had remembered the quilt, I had not paid much attention to the details of the print. It lacked significant value to me because the quilt top was only one piece of Christmas printed fabric rather than the individually pieced quilt blocks Mom usually sewed.

Remembering Rose's dream, I decided to unfold the quilt to examine it. To my astonishment, printed pink and red roses mingled in the design of the fabric! Christmas trees alternated with stars along the border. I picked up the quilt and held it close, wiping away my tears. I felt assured that all was well with my mother in heaven.

This experience gave me a glimpse of God's compassion. He revealed to me that Mom and I both reside in the presence of the true Comforter. We are just in different locations of His kingdom.

Chapter 16

The Bells Rang for Joy

The rain pelted down on the sidewalk as I scurried into the church for the weekly healing service. When I entered, I noticed everyone gathering in the choir loft of the main sanctuary. Usually the service was held in the chapel, but that morning the rector had detected an "undiagnosed racket" and relocated the service. A beautiful cathedral ceiling and magnificent stained-glass windows surrounded us, which seemed quite fitting for that particular day.

Mixed emotions weighed heavily on my heart that morning, for just the day before, Dr. Rev. Rufus Womble had gone to be with Jesus. During the service, when the rector asked us to share one word that we felt described Rufus, I listened in agreement with the many words spoken—humble, loving, caring, kind, and sincere; on and on the endearing words came. Rufus' wife said, "Joy." As the service continued, I thought about the word *joy*. Rufus' Christ-like behavior continually revealed the joy, love, and hope that he knew Christ wanted each of us to have.

Every Thursday evening at the dinner table, my husband and daughter asked me what Rufus' message and jokes had been that morning. Since my memory often fails me in the midst of attempting to repeat what I've heard, I had begun to take notes on Rufus' powerful messages—and his jokes! Each week during the service, Rufus offered us all a dose of risotherapy, healing through laughter, by sharing three jokes. On this day, although I did not write any notes, I took mental ones. I remember the words from the prayer book as they were read during the service, "Receive our brother, Rufus, into the courts of your heavenly dwelling place. Let his heart and soul now ring out in joy to You, O Lord." At the very moment those words were spoken, the 11:00 bells began chiming. I couldn't help but laugh. I could imagine Jesus with Rufus in heaven orchestrating the perfect timing for the bells to ring, once again bringing us risotherapy to heal our sad hearts. The earlier heaviness I felt when I walked through the church doors totally dissolved.

The memories of joy, love, and hope that Rufus shared will remain with me for years to come. And one day when we meet the Lord face to face, we will all get to hear those bells ring for joy!

Chapter 17

Without a Doubt

Dear Lord,

Thank You for promising that if we seek You with all our heart, we will find You.

Thank You for wanting to guide us through life and untangling the weeds from our path, freeing us to follow You.

Thank You for helping us shake off any bitterness and resentment we have toward others, forgiving them as You have forgiven us.

When clouds come our way, thank You for allowing us to see the sun's rays bursting through, unveiling Your Presence.

Thank You for comforting us through the heartbreaks of life with Your blanket of compassion.

During challenging seasons, thank You for nurturing our growth and enabling us to fully bloom.

In the midst of the clamoring world, thank You for the rest You give us and the peace You want us to accept.

Thank You for taking us up to the mountain tops to see Your glory through glimpses and signs of Your presence.

Thank You for assuring us that, without a doubt, You will continue to reveal Yourself to us in ways we cannot imagine.

Thank You for Your love, dear Lord. Amen.

Notes

Chapter 1
1. Exodus 13:21-22 NIV
2. Jeremiah 29:13 NIV

Chapter 3
1. 1 Corinthians 13:4 NIV

Chapter 4
1. Mark 9:2 NKJV
2. Oswald Chambers, *My Utmost for His Highest,* (Grand Rapids, MI: Discovery House Publishers, 1992), October 1.

Chapter 5
1. Psalm 121:1-2 NIV

Chapter 6
1. Hebrews 12:1 LB
2. Nehemiah 8:10 NIV
3. 1 Peter 2:24 KJV

Chapter 8
1. Matthew 18:19-20 NIV

Chapter 13
1. Psalm 62:1-2 NIV
2. Hebrews 11:1 NIV

Chapter 15
1. 2 Kings 20:3 NIV
2. 2 Kings 20:5 NIV
3. Ruth 1:16 KJV
4. Luke 10:41 NIV
5. C. S. Lewis, *Mere Christianity* (New York, NY: Harper Collins Publishers, Inc., 2001), 136-137.
6. John 11:4 NIV
7. Psalm 84:1-4
8. Galatians 6:9 NIV